WEEKEND MAKES

STASH KNITTING

25 QUICK AND EASY PROJECTS TO MAKE

WEEKEND MAKES

STASH KNITTING

25 QUICK AND EASY PROJECTS TO MAKE

EMMA OSMOND

THE GUILD OF MASTER CRAFTSMAN
PUBLICATIONS

First published 2019 by
Guild of Master Craftsman Publications Ltd Castle Place,
166 High Street, Lewes,
East Sussex, BN7 1XU

Text © Emma Osmond, 2019
Copyright in the Work © GMC Publications Ltd, 2019

ISBN 978-1-78494-512-1

A catalogue record for this book is available from the
British Library.

Senior Project Editor: Kandy Regis
Managing Art Editor: Darren Brant
Art Editor: Lindsay Birch
Photographer: Jesse Wild
Stylist: Georgina Brant

Colour origination by GMC Reprographics
Printed and bound in China

CONTENTS

Introduction

If you're a knitter, then chances are, you'll have a little hoard of leftover bits and pieces of yarn or balls of some favourite collectables that you've bought over time and hidden away, with every intention of making use of them one day. It's a well-known guilty pleasure that all yarn lovers can relate to.

Working with so many gorgeous yarns on a daily basis, I have a huge stash yarn room and so I have taken inspiration from my own dilemma to create *Stash Knitting*, a bumper pattern collection of 25 super cool knitting patterns that will have you reaching for your needles.

By deliberately not straying from my signature pared-down style, the collection offers some lovely projects for items that we all use every day, from a mitred-corner cushion that will add a touch of comfort to the home, stylish must-have accessories for the chillier months of the year, to adorable gifts for the baby that any new mum would love to receive – all in my modern, less is more style.

So, whether you're a newbie to the craft or you're looking for something a bit trickier to keep you interested, I have it covered and all from only using just a small amount of yarn found in your own store cupboard to knit something fresh and lovely that you'll want to show off.

Emma Osmond

Stash knitting

With so many gorgeous yarns now available to us, it really takes some effort not to be tempted into buying more than you need for a particular project 'just because' it's so lovely, or simply 'just in case'. It takes a strong-willed knitter to walk away from a beautiful quality yarn that they simply don't think they can live without – even if they have no idea what they want to make with it, let alone have a pattern so it's inevitable that many of us end up with a stash of yarns squirrelled away waiting to be used.

MAKING THE MOST OF YOUR STASH

Unless you've bought a number of balls in a particular yarn, much of your stash probably consists of parts of balls from projects that didn't take quite as much as the pattern stated, whilst thrifty knitters might have saved even smaller amounts of leftovers. Whatever you've got in your hoard, here are a few steps to make the most of it:

1 Group the yarns into their type, look for the same texture and fibre content, for example wool or cotton etc. You can get this information from the ball band – it's always a good idea to make a habit of storing one with each of your leftovers, or keep your ball bands in a notebook with a little piece of yarn by their side. As fibres work differently from each other – wool being stretchy, cotton firm – this will determine the finished fabric.

2 Sort each group into thicknesses – match yarns that share the same standard tension and size of needles to achieve this.

3 If you're using whole balls of yarn from your stash, they will more than likely be a different yarn to that which is quoted in the pattern, so do check the meterage because yarns of the same weight may still have different lengths in the ball or hank and so you may need more or less than suggested. Check the ball band for the length and, if it's different, work out the amount needed by multiplying the length of the yarn used by the amount of balls quoted, divide this figure by the number of metres stated on the yarn you wish to use and that will give you the number of balls you need.

4 Finally, chances are your yarn stash will have a particular theme running through it, as you'll have particular favourites that you always sway towards, perhaps it's a texture or a certain colour palette – yarns grouped together in a similar collection can look stunning and so inspiring. Yarns are dyed in batches or lots, which can vary, so it's important to always check lot numbers of yarns of the shade that you wish to use in a project. Even a little variation could make a big difference to your finished piece.

CHOOSING YARNS

Once you've got some order into your yarn collection, it's time for the fun bit - deciding what it is you'd like to knit. Firstly, I always consider the yarn and its fibre as a starting point for any project. With yarns that vary from whisper-thin to gigantically fat being available, the yarn must be suitable for its purpose because this determines the stitch and texture of the final finished fabric. So, for this book, I have carefully considered yarns that would be generally found in an average stash cupboard before pairing them with an appropriate project idea.

TECHNIQUES

Cables

Many knitters avoid cabling as it looks complex, but just try it and you will see that it is deceptive and is really quite a simple technique to master. Cables are stitches that have been lifted with a third needle and crossed to another place in the work, and it's the third needle that puts people off. The actual cables are usually worked in stocking stitch on a background of reverse stocking stitch or sometimes moss stitch.

All cables use the techniques shown, but they can involve different numbers of stitches. For example, 'C6B' means 'cable six back'. You would slip three stitches onto the cable needle and hold it at the back, then knit three from the left-hand needle and finally the three from the cable needle. The pattern you are working from will tell you how many stitches to put on the cable needle and how many to knit.

CABLE 4 BACK (C4B)

1 Work to the position of the cable. Slip the first two stitches from the left-hand needle onto the cable needle and leave it at the back of the work.

2 Coming in front of the needle that is holding the two stitches, knit the next two stitches from the left-hand needle.

3 Now knit the two stitches from the cable needle to complete the cable four back. If you find that the first stitch purled after the cable needle is baggy, try purling into the back of it to tighten it.

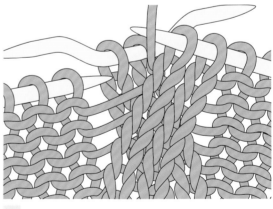

1

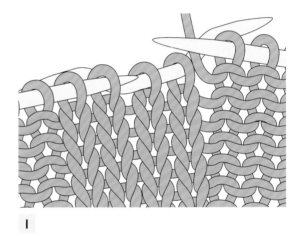

2

CABLE 4 FRONT (C4F)

Holding the cable needle at the front of the work makes the cable twist across to the left.

1 Work to the position of the cable. Slip the first two stitches from the left-hand needle onto the cable needle and leave it at the front of the work.

2 Going behind the cable needle that is holding the stitches, knit the next two stitches from the left-hand needle.

3 Then knit the two stitches that are on the cable needle to complete the cable.

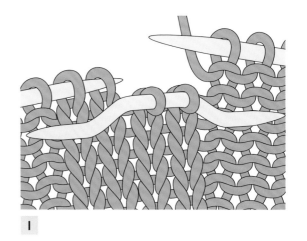

1

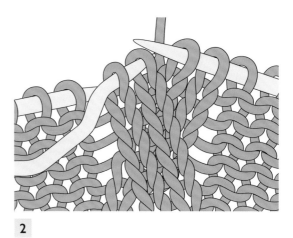

2

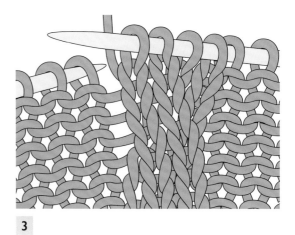

3

Intarsia knitting

Intarsia is colour work where the fabric remains single-thickness throughout. You have to join the areas of colour that are next to each other as you work. Like all new techniques it takes practice, but it is one of the most enjoyable types of knitting. The intarsia technique is used to knit individual motifs where the background colour remains the same on either side.

JOINING IN A NEW COLOUR

When working in intarsia you will find yourself needing to join in a new colour in the middle of a row.

1 On a knit row, knit to the change in colour. Lay the new colour over the existing colour and between the two needles, with the tail to the left.

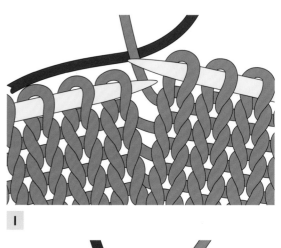

2 Bring the new colour under and then over the existing colour.

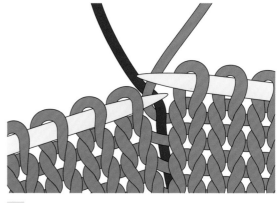

3 Knit the stitch with the new colour. Go back and pull gently on the tail to tighten up the first stitch in the new colour after you have knitted a couple more stitches.

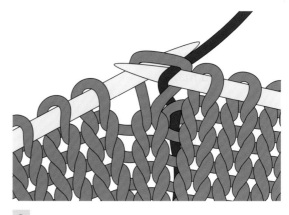

CHANGING COLOURS IN A STRAIGHT VERTICAL LINE

Once you have joined in a new colour you may need to work for a number of rows changing these colours on both the knit rows and purl rows.

This is often confusingly referred to as 'twisting' the yarns but it is a link rather than a twist. It is a common mistake to over-twist the yarns at this point and then the fabric will not lie flat.

1 On a knit row, knit to the change in colour. Bring the new colour up from under the old colour and drop the old colour so that the new colour is ready to work with.

2 On a purl row, knit to the change in colour. Bring the new colour from the left under the old colour and up to the top. Drop the old colour and continue with the new colour.

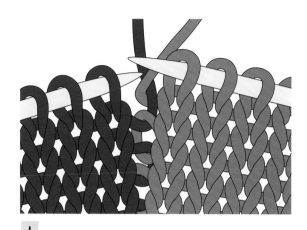

1

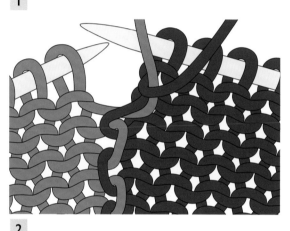

2

CHANGING COLOURS ON THE DIAGONAL

The technique is the same as for changing colours in a straight line (above), but you will find that sometimes the yarn you want is in a different place and if you get the technique wrong you may end up over-twisting the yarns.

1 On a knit row with the diagonal going to the right, bring the new colour from underneath the old colour and knit with it.

1

2 On a purl row with the diagonal going to the left, bring the new colour from underneath the old colour and purl with it.

3 On a purl row with the diagonal going to the right, bring the new colour under the old colour and purl with it.

4 On a knit row with the diagonal going to the left, bring the new colour from underneath the old colour and knit with it.

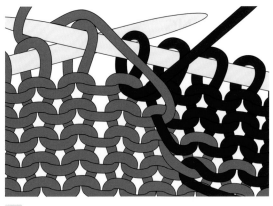

2

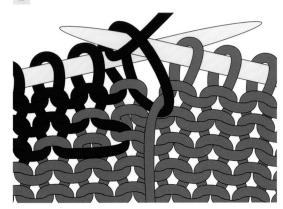

3

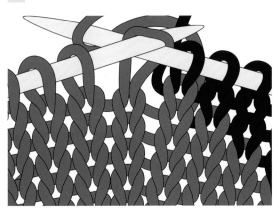

4

BRINGING A COLOUR ACROSS THE BACK

When working in intarsia you will sometimes need to carry a contrast yarn across the back for a few stitches, ready for the next row where it will be needed earlier than where it was left on the previous row. You can do this by weaving in the contrast yarn along the row, but if you have missed doing this, there is another technique.

1 On a purl row, bring the contrast colour across the stitches to where it is needed, keeping the loop quite loose. Bring it under the original colour and purl a stitch with the contrast colour.

2 To anchor the contrast loop as you purl across the row, put the tip of the right-hand needle into the next stitch and then under the loop.

3 Purl the stitch, making sure that the loop doesn't go through the stitch. Repeat on every alternate stitch until the loop is anchored across the fabric.

4 Here you can see the back of a knit row and the dark purple yarn that needs to come across the stitches.

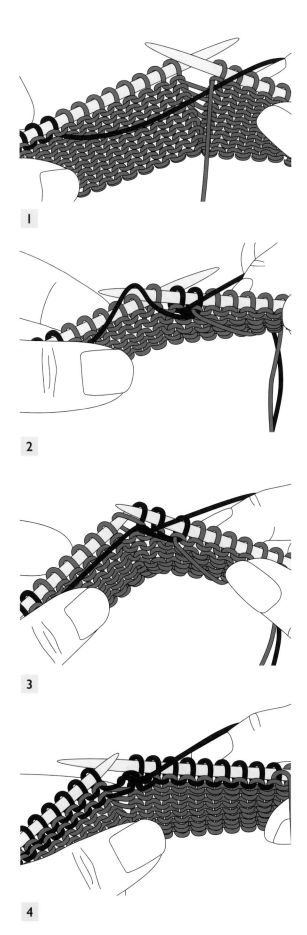

1

2

3

4

5 Bring the yarn across the back of the stitches to where it is needed, keeping the loop quite loose, and knit the stitch with it.

6 To anchor the loop as you knit across the row, put the tip of the right-hand needle into the next stitch and then under the back of the loop. Knit with the new colour, not allowing the loop to come through the stitch. Repeat on every alternate stitch until the loop is anchored across the fabric.

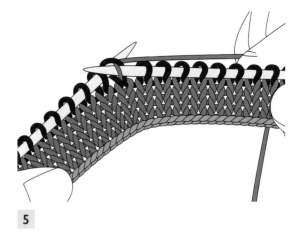

5

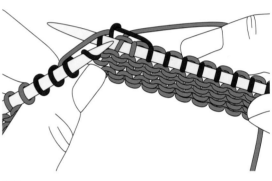

6

Fair Isle

With this type of colour knitting you are working with one or more colours in stocking stitch and the pattern is a repetitive design. Yarns that are not being used will have to be carried (or stranded, as it is known), across the back of the work, thus making the fabric double thickness. The art of good Fair Isle is to keep the fabric elastic and supple and to achieve this you must be careful not to pull the yarns too tightly. When worked properly the yarns should not tangle.

Once you have joined in the yarns, there are three possible techniques to use when knitting in Fair Isle and they all take practice to master. The techniques differ in whether you hold the yarns only in your right hand or in both hands. Whichever technique you use, it is advisable to only strand the yarn across the back for a maximum of three stitches. If the design requires you to carry the yarn for more than three stitches then you need to catch the yarn into the back of the work. If you do not do this you will end up with large loops that you will catch your fingers in as you put the garment on. You will also tend to pull the strands too tight and this will cause the work to pucker on the front.

JOINING IN A NEW COLOUR ON A KNIT ROW

When working Fair Isle, it is better to join in a new colour at the beginning of a row, but if you have to join it in mid row, this is how to do it on a knit row.

1 Lay the new colour (B) over the original colour (A). Twist the yarns over themselves and hold them in place.

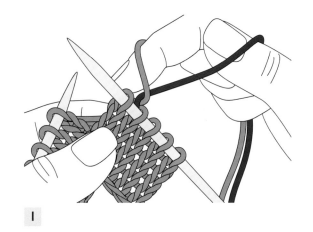

1

2 Knit with the new colour (B). You can always go back and tighten the join after a couple of stitches.

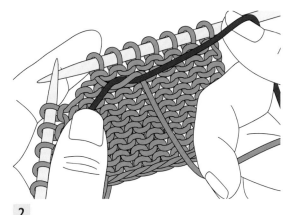

2

JOINING IN A NEW COLOUR ON A PURL ROW

This is how you join in a new colour mid-row on a purl row.

1 Lay the new colour (B) over the original colour (A). Twist the yarns over themselves and hold them in place.

2 Purl with the new colour (B).

1

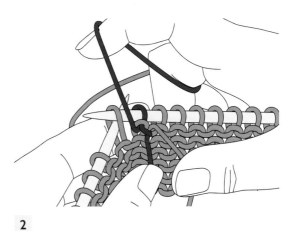

2

Working in the round

CIRCULAR KNITTING

The easiest way to knit in the round is to use a circular needle. It has two pointed ends joined with a cord, usually made from plastic or nylon. A circular needle enables you to knit a tube with no side seams to sew up. You can knit a sweater this way up to the armholes, then you will have to divide the front and back. This is particularly useful when knitting in a complicated Fair Isle pattern, as it makes it easier to match the pattern at the side seams. Another place where circular knitting is useful is on a neckband, especially a polo neck, as working in the round eliminates any seams. Some knitters also find it an advantage that you only work in the stitch making the right side of the fabric, usually knit stitch.

Circular needles come in different lengths and a pattern should tell you which length to use. Using the two pointed tips of the circular needle, cast on in the usual way. If the needle is the right length, the cast on stitches should fill it without having to stretch them out (which can make the knitting hard work or impossible).

1 Once you have cast on the correct number of stitches, check carefully that the cast on row is not twisted around the needle. If it is, you will end up knitting a Mobius strip, which can be fun for a scarf but is useless for a sweater.

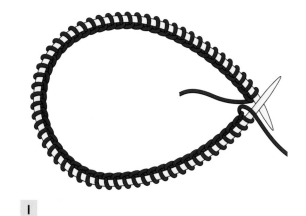

I

2 Place a round marker on right-hand point of the needle after you have cast on the correct number of stitches. When knitting the first stitch that was cast on, make sure you pull it tight to prevent a hole forming.

2

3 Knit until you come to the marker; you have completed one round. Slip the marker onto the right-hand point of the needle and knit the next round.

DOUBLE-POINTED NEEDLES

Double-pointed needles can also be used to work in the round and create a tube of knitting. Novice knitters are often put off knitting in this way because of the extra needles, but there is no need to be. You are still only knitting on two needles at any one time and after a bit of practice you will find that you can just ignore those you are not actually using.

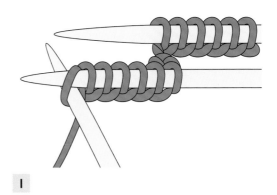

You can choose to work on four or five needles; usually you would work on four needles on a small project, like a sock, and for larger projects you would use five needles. The example shown here uses four needles. You need to divide the number of stitches between three of the needles and the fourth will be the needle you knit with.

1 Cast on the required number of stitches onto the first needle, plus one extra stitch. Slip the extra stitch onto the second needle then repeat the process until the required number of stitches is cast on to all the needles.

2 Lay out the needles with the tips overlapping as shown here. Make sure that the cast-on edge faces into the middle of the triangle all the way around and is not twisted at any point.

3 Place a round marker on the needle after the last stitch has been cast on. Using the free needle, knit the stitches off the first needle. When all the stitches are knitted, the first needle becomes the free one, ready to knit the stitches off the second needle with. Continue knitting off each needle in turn until you come to the marker and then slip the marker from the left-hand needle to the right-hand needle and knit the next round.

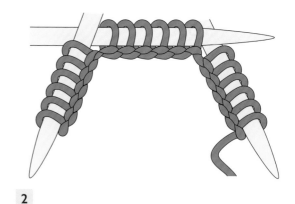

2

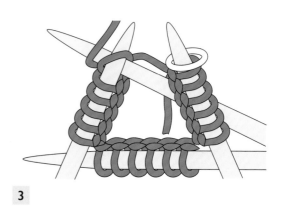

3

Swiss darning

Swiss darning resembles knit stitches and can be used to add small areas of colour detail without all the fuss of knitting with several colours. It may also be used to hide a mistake in your colour knitting.

1 To work a horizontal row of Swiss darning, work from right to left across the knitted fabric. Bring the needle through from the back of the fabric at the base of a stitch then take it under the two loops at the base of the stitch above.

2 Put the needle back through to the back of the fabric where it first came out at the base of the lower stitch and take it across to come out at the base of the next stitch to the left. One Swiss-darned stitch is complete.

3 To work a vertical row, work from bottom to top of the knitted fabric. Bring the needle through the base of a stitch and take it under the loops of the stitch above, as before.

Take it back through the base of the stitch and the bring it to the front through the base of the stitch above.

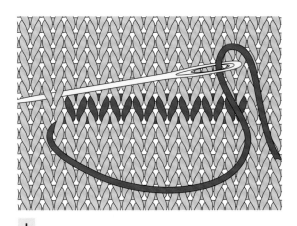

1

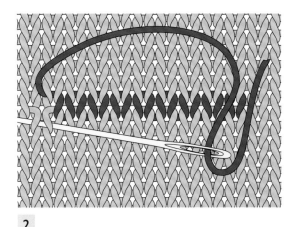

2

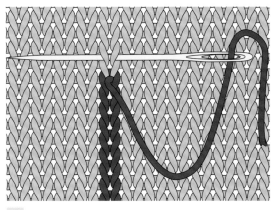

3

PATTERNS

CABLED BEANIE

This cabled beanie is a great project to use up any of your chunkier yarns. The cable detail is really eye catching and with its turn back brim makes the perfect statement piece. Accompany your beanie design with a colour coordinating faux fur pompom, or simply make a woollen one by using some of your stash yarn.

SKILL LEVEL: SOME EXPERIENCE

YOU'LL NEED:

YARN
106g / 122m of Rowan Cocoon or any No.5 Bulky weight yarn (photographed in Frost 806)

NEEDLES
6mm (no 4) (US 10) needles
7mm (no 2) (US 10.5/11) needles

EXTRAS
Pompom – we used a Rowan faux fur pompom

CABLED BEANIE

SIZE

To fit an average size adult woman's head

TENSION

18sts and 20 rows to 10cm/4in
Measured over cable pattern using 7mm
(US 10.5/11) needles.

SPECIAL ABBREVIATIONS

C4B – slip next 2 stitches onto a cable
needle, hold at back of work, knit next
2 stitches, knit 2 stitches from cable needle.
C4F – slip next 2 stitches onto a cable
needle, hold at front of work, knit next
2 stitches, knit 2 stitches from cable needle.
C6B – slip next 3 stitches onto a cable
needle, hold at back of work, knit next
3 stitches, knit 3 stitches from cable needle.

HAT

Using 6mm (US 10) needles cast on
74 stitches.

Row 1: Knit 1, purl 1 to end.
Last row sets rib pattern.
Work in rib pattern until work measures
6.5cm/2½in, ending with a right side row.
Next Row: (WS) Increase 6 stitches evenly
along next row in rib pattern. 80 stitches.
Change to 7mm (US 10.5/11) needles
Row 1: (RS) * Purl 2, knit 4, C4B, C4F,
knit 4, purl 2, knit 6 repeat from * to last
2 stitches, purl 2.
Row 2: Knit 2 * purl 6, knit 2, purl 16,
knit 2 repeat from * to end.
Row 3: * Purl 2, knit 2, C4B, knit 4, C4F, knit 2,
purl 2 C6B repeat from * to last 2 stitches, purl 2.
Row 4: Knit 2 * purl 6, knit 2, purl 16,
knit 2 repeat from * to end.
Row 5: * Purl 2, C4B, knit 8, C4F, purl 2, knit
6 repeat from * to last 2 stitches, purl 2.
Row 6: Knit 2 * purl 6, knit 2, purl 16, knit 2
repeat from * to end.
Rep last 6 rows, 5 times more.

SHAPE CROWN

Row 37: (RS) * Purl 2, C4B, knit 2 together, knit 4, knit 2 together, C4F, purl 2, knit 2, kit 2 together, knit 2 repeat from * to last 2 stitches, purl 2. 71 stitches.

Row 38: Knit 2, * purl 5, knit 2, purl 14, knit 2 repeat from * to end.

Row 39: * Purl 2, knit 2 together, knit 1, C4B, C4F, knit 1, knit 2 together, purl 2, knit 2, knit 2 together, knit 1 repeat from * to last 2 stitches, purl 2. 62 stitches.

Row 40: Knit 2, * purl 4, knit 2, purl 12, knit 2 repeat from * to end.

Row 41: * Purl 2, C4B, (knit 2 together) twice, C4F, purl 2, knit 1, knit 2 together, knit 1 repeat from * to last 2 stitches, purl 2. 53 stitches.

Row 42: Knit 2, * purl 3, knit 2, purl 10, knit 2 repeat from * to end.

Row 43: * Purl 2, knit 2, knit 2 together, knit 2, knit 2 together, knit 2, purl 2, knit 3 together repeat from * to last 2 stitches, purl 2. 41 stitches.

Row 44: Knit 2 * purl 1, knit 2, purl 8, knit 2, repeat from * to end.

Row 45: * Purl 2, (knit 2 together) four times, purl 2, knit 1 repeat from * to last 2 stitches, purl 2. 29 stitches.

Row 46: * Knit 2 together, purl 1, knit 2 together, (purl 2 together) twice repeat from * to last 2 stitches, knit 2 together. 16 stitches.

MAKING UP

Press as described on the information page (see page 140).

Cut yarn, leaving a long enough tail to sew up hat. Pull yarn through remaining stitches and join seam using mattress stitch (see page 134) reversing for turn up. Attach pompom.

BABY BOOTIES

These beautifully constructed baby booties are the perfect footwear choice for a new addition to a family. Use a super soft yarn for those delicate little feet, and keep them nice and warm with the turn over tops.

SKILL LEVEL: EASY

YOU'LL NEED:

YARN
25g / 68m of Rowan Baby Merino Silk DK or any No.3 light-weight yarn (photographed in Dawn 672)

NEEDLES
4mm (no 8) (US 6) needles
4 x 3.75mm (no 9) (US 5) double-pointed needles

BABY BOOTIES

SIZE

0 – 3 months

TENSION

22 stitches and 30 rows to 10cm/4in
Measured over stocking stitch using 4mm
(US 6) needles

BOOTIES – MAKE TWO

Using 4mm (US 6) needles cast on 6 stitches.
Next Row: (RS) Knit.
Next Row: Knit 1, make 1, knit to last stitch,
make 1, knit 1. 8 stitches.
Repeat last 2 rows once more. 10 stitches.
Continue in garter stitch until work measures
8cm/3¼in, ending with a wrong side row.
Next Row: (RS) Knit 1, knit 2 together,
knit to last 3 stitches, knit 2 together,
knit 1. 8 stitches.
Next Row: Knit.
Repeat last 2 rows once more. 6 stitches.
Do not break off yarn.

Using 3.75mm (US 5) double-pointed
needles pick up and knit 46 stitches evenly
around sole. 52 stitches.
Arrange 17 stitches on the first 2 needles
and 18 on the third.
Round 1: Purl.
Round 2 – 6: Knit.
Round 7: Knit 23 stitches, place marker, knit
to end.
Round 8: Knit to 6 stitches before stitch
marker, (knit 2 together) 3 times, slip marker,
(knit 2 together) 3 times, knit to end.
46 stitches.
Round 9: Knit.
Repeat last 2 rounds twice more. 34 stitches.
Next Round: *Knit 1, purl 1 repeat
from * to end.
Repeat last round until rib measures
6cm/2¼in.
Cast off in pattern.

MAKING UP

Press as described on the information page
(see page 140).

CABLED CUSHION

Add texture and interest to any room with this intricate cable cushion. The cable stitch is really fun to create and produces a honeycomb effect. Adding a fabric back enables you to easily customize the cushion to work with the décor of the room of your choice.

SKILL LEVEL: SOME EXPERIENCE

YOU'LL NEED:

YARN
185g / 500m of Rowan Softyak DK or any No.3 light-weight yarn (photographed in Taupe 245)

NEEDLES
4mm (no 8) (US 6) needles

EXTRAS
Cable needle.
Cushion pad 50cm x 50cm / 20in x 20in.
Two pieces of fabric for backing measuring 55cm x 55cm / 21¾in x 21¾in if making your own cushion cover or a premade cushion cover measuring 50cm x 50cm / 20in x 20in.

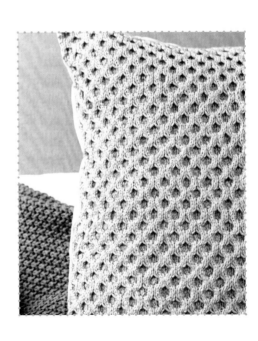

CABLED CUSHION

SIZE
50cm x 50cm / 20in x 20in

TENSION
34 stitches and 30 rows to 10cm/4in
Measured over cable pattern using 4mm
(US 6) needles

SPECIAL ABBREVIATIONS
C4B – slip next 2 stitches onto a cable
needle and hold at back of work knit 2
stitches, knit 2 stitches from cable needle.
C4F – slip next 2 stitches onto a cable
needle and hold at front of work knit 2
stitches, knit 2 stitches from cable needle.

CUSHION
Using 4mm (US 6) needles cast on 168
stitches.
Row 1: (RS) Knit.
Row 2: (WS) Purl.
Row 3: *C4B, C4F repeat from * to end.
Row 4: Purl.
Row 5: Knit
Row 6: Purl.
Row 7: * C4F, C4B repeat from * to end.
Row 8: Purl.
Last 8 rows set pattern.
Work in pattern until work measures
50cm/20in, ending on row 8 of pattern.
Cast off knitwise.

MAKING UP
Press as described on the information page
(see page 140).
We chose to make our own cushion cover
by placing the wrong sides of fabric together,
using a 2.5cm/1in seam allowance sew 3 of
the 4 sides together. Turn right way out and
press open seam 2.5cm/1in inwards. Hand
stitch knitted cover to one of the pieces.
Stitch final seam encasing the cushion pad.

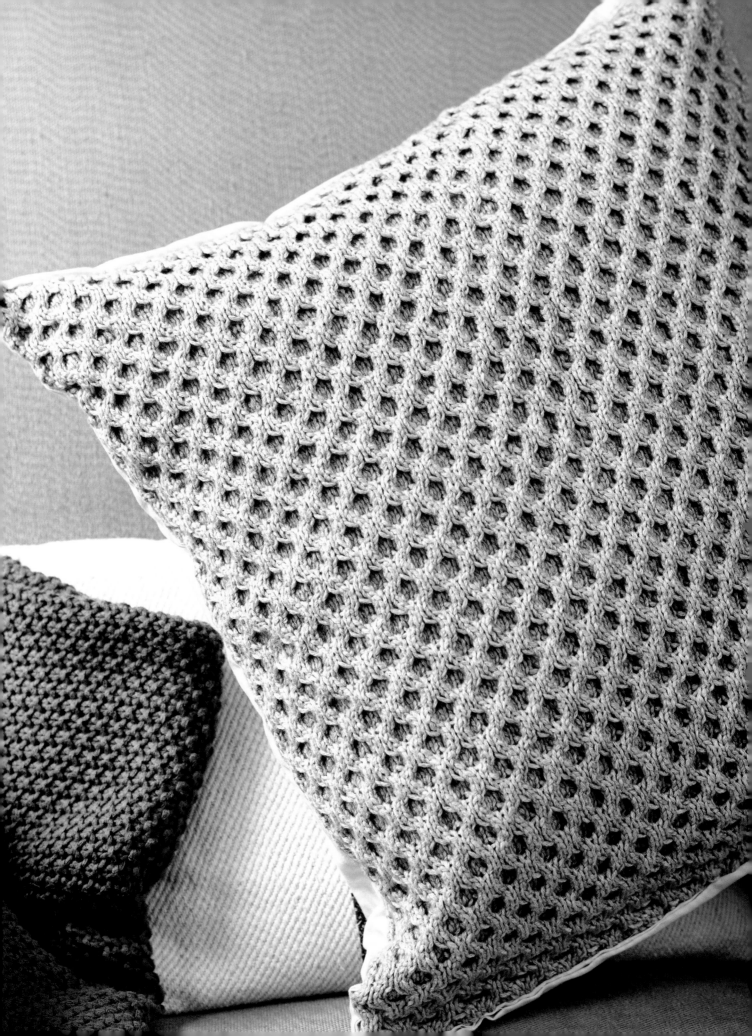

CHEVRON BLANKET

This blanket is a great way to use up small amounts of yarn that you may have within your stash. Blending colour tones enables you to really make the blanket your own and suit the different rooms in your home.

SKILL LEVEL: SOME EXPERIENCE

YOU'LL NEED:

YARN
Rowan Handknit Cotton or any No.3
light-weight yarn
(A) 128g / 218m of North Sea 371
(B) 90g / 153m of Ecru 251
(C) 90g / 153m of Celery 309
(D) 90g / 153m of Gooseberry 219
(E) 90g / 153m of Forest 370
(F) 90g / 153m of Sunshine 354
(G) 90g / 153m of Slate 347
(H) 90g / 153m of Sea Foam 352

NEEDLES
5mm (no 6) (US 8) needles

CHEVRON BLANKET

SIZE
94.5cm x 120cm / 37¼in x 47¼in

TENSION
18 stitches and 20 rows to 10cm/4in
Measured over pattern using 5mm
(US 8) needles.

SPECIAL ABBREVIATIONS
KFB – Knit into the front and back of the stitch.
SSK – Slip next stitch as if to knit, slip next stitch as if to knit, insert left hand needle into front of 2 slipped stitches and knit.

BLANKET
Using yarn A and 5mm (US 8) needles cast on 170 stitches.
Row 1: (WS) Purl.
Row 2: Knit 1, Kfb, knit4, SSK, knit 2 together, knit4, * Kfb twice, knit 4, SSK, knit 2 together, knit 4 repeat from * to last 2 stitches, Kfb, knit 1.
Last 2 rows set pattern.

Work in pattern for 10 rows more.
Change to yarn B.
Row 13: Purl.
Row 14: Knit 1, Kfb, knit 4, SSK, knit 2 together, knit 4, * Kfb twice, knit 4, SSK, knit 2 together, knit 4 repeat from * to last 2 stitches, Kfb, knit 1.
Work in pattern for 10 rows more.
Change to yarn C.
Row 25: Purl.
Row 26: Knit 1, Kfb, knit 4, SSK, knit 2 together, knit 4, * Kfb twice, knit 4, SSK, knit 2 together, knit 4 repeat from * to last 2 stitches, Kfb, knit 1.
Work in pattern for 10 rows more.
Change to yarn D.
Row 37: Purl.
Row 38: Knit 1, Kfb, knit 4, SSK, knit 2 together, knit 4, * Kfb twice, knit 4, SSK, knit 2 together, knit 4 repeat from * to last 2 stitches, Kfb, knit 1.
Work in pattern for 10 rows more.

Change to yarn E.

Row 49: Purl.

Row 50: Knit 1, Kfb, knit 4, SSK, knit 2 together, knit 4, * Kfb twice, knit 4, SSK, knit 2 together, knit 4 repeat from * to last 2 stitches, Kfb, knit 1.

Work in pattern for 10 rows more.

Change to yarn F.

Row 61: Purl.

Row 62: Knit 1, Kfb, knit 4, SSK, knit 2 together, knit 4, * Kfb twice, knit 4, SSK, knit 2 together, knit 4 repeat from * to last 2 stitches, Kfb, knit 1.

Work in pattern for 10 rows more.

Change to yarn G.

Row 73: Purl.

Row 74: Knit 1, Kfb, knit 4, SSK, knit 2 together, knit 4, * Kfb twice, knit 4, SSK, knit 2 together, knit 4 repeat from * to last 2 stitches, Kfb, knit 1.

Work in pattern for 10 rows more.

Change to yarn H.

Repeat rows 1 – 84, 2 times more.

Change to yarn A.

Row 253: Purl.

Row 254: Knit 1, Kfb, knit 4, SSK, knit 2 together, knit 4, * Kfb twice, knit 4, SSK, knit 2 together, knit 4 repeat from * to last 2 stitches, Kfb, knit 1.

Work in pattern for 10 rows more.

Cast off.

MAKING UP

Press as described on the information page (see page 140).

CHUNKY LACE SNOOD

This simple lace snood is a great way of using your chunky stash yarns, the simple eyelets add a point of interest and challenge your knitting skills at the same time. If you wanted to make the snood longer then you could just repeat the pattern, using more of your stash yarn.

SKILL LEVEL: SOME EXPERIENCE

YOU'LL NEED:

YARN
200g / 160m of Rowan Big Wool or any
No.6 Super Bulky weight yarn
(photographed in Concrete 61)

NEEDLES
12mm (no 0) (US 17) needles

CHUNKY LACE SNOOD

SIZE
36cm x 96cm / 14¼in x 37¾in

TENSION
8 stitches and 12 rows to 10cm/4in
Measured over stocking stitch using 12mm
(US 17) needles

SNOOD
Using 12mm (US 17) needles cast on
29 stitches.
Row 1: (RS) Knit.
Row 2 and all even numbered rows:
Knit 3, purl 23, knit 3.
Row 3: Knit 12, knit 2 together, yarn forward,
knit 1, yarn forward, slip 1, knit 1, pass slipped
stitch over, knit 12.
Row 5: Knit 13, yarn forward, slip 1, knit
2 together, pass slipped stitch over, yarn
forward, knit 13.
Row 7: Knit 9, knit 2 together, yarn forward,
knit 1, yarn forward, slip 1, knit 1, pass slipped

stitch over, knit 1, knit 2 together, yarn
forward, knit 1, yarn forward, slip 1, knit 1,
pass slipped stitch over, knit 9.
Row 9: Knit 10, yarn forward, slip 1, knit
2 together, pass slipped stitch over, yarn
forward, knit 3, yarn forward, slip 1, knit
2 together, pass slipped stitch over, yarn
forward, knit 10.
Row 11: Knit 6, knit 2 together, (yarn
forward, knit 1, yarn forward, slip 1, knit
1, pass slipped stitch over, knit 1, knit 2
together) twice, yarn forward, knit 1, yarn
forward, slip 1, knit 1, pass slipped stitch over,
knit 6.
Row 13: Knit 7, yarn forward, slip 1, knit
2 together, pass slipped stitch over, yarn
forward, knit 1, knit 2 together, yarn forward,
knit 3, yarn forward, slip 1, knit 1, pass slipped
stitch over, knit 1, yarn forward, slip 1, knit
2 together, pass slipped stitch over, yarn
forward, knit 7.
Row 15: Knit 3, knit 2 together, yarn forward,

knit 1, yarn forward, slip 1, knit 1, pass slipped stitch over, knit 2, knit 2 together, yarn forward, knit 5, yarn forward, slip 1, knit 1, pass slipped stitch over, knit 2, knit 2 together, yarn forward, knit 1, yarn forward, slip 1, knit 1, pass slipped stitch over, knit 3.

Row 17: Knit 4, yarn forward, slip 1, knit 2 together, pass slipped stitch over, yarn forward, knit 4, yarn forward, slip 1, knit 1, pass slipped stitch over, knit 3, knit 2 together, yarn forward, knit 4, yarn forward, slip 1, knit 2 together, pass slipped stitch over, yarn forward, knit 4.

Row 19: Knit 6, knit 2 together, (yarn forward, knit 1) twice, slip 1, knit 1, pass slipped stitch over, yarn forward, slip 1, knit 1, pass slipped stitch over, knit 1, knit 2 together, yarn forward, knit 2 together, (knit 1, yarn forward) twice, slip 1, knit 1, pass slipped stitch over, knit 6.

Row 21: Knit 7, (yarn forward, slip 1, knit 2 together, pass slipped stitch over, yarn forward, knit 3) three times, knit 4.

Row 23: Knit 9, knit 2 together, yarn forward, knit 1, yarn forward, slip 1, knit 1, pass slipped stitch over, knit 1, knit 2 together, yarn forward, knit 1, yarn forward, slip 1, knit 1, pass slipped stitch over, knit 9.

Row 25: Knit 10, yarn forward, slip 1, knit 2 together, pass slipped stitch over, yarn forward, knit 3, yarn forward, slip 1, knit 2 together, pass slipped stitch over, yarn forward, knit 10.

Row 27: Knit 12, knit 2 together, yarn forward, knit 1, yarn forward, slip 1, knit 1, pass slipped stitch over, knit 12.

Row 29: Knit 13, yarn forward, slip 1, knit 2 together, pass slipped stitch over, yarn forward, knit 13.

Row 30: Knit 3, purl 23, knit 3.
Repeat rows 1 – 30 twice more, then rows 1 – 22 once.
Row 113: Knit.
Row 114: Knit 3, purl 23, knit 3.
Cast off loosely.

MAKING UP

Press as described on the information page (see page 140).
Join cast on and cast off edges using mattress stitch (see page 134).

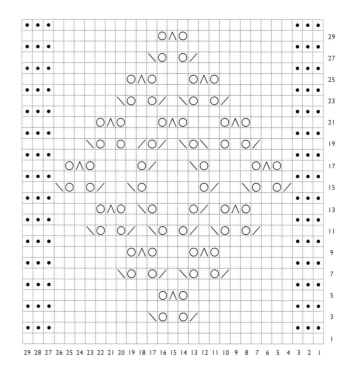

Key

□ RS: knit WS: purl	○ yfwd
● RS: purl WS: knit	＼ sl1, k1, psso
／ RS: k2tog WS: p2tog	∧ sl1, k2tog, psso

COLOUR BLOCK SCARF

This is a really fun scarf to make and you could make it in a range of colours, each producing a completely different looking scarf. Using a simple garter slip stitch creates a neat fabric that is perfect for wrapping up in.

SKILL LEVEL: EASY

YOU'LL NEED:

YARN

Rowan Baby Merino Silk DK or any No.3
Light weight yarn
(A) 124g / 335m of Dawn 672
(B) 50g / 135m of Teal 677
(C) 50g / 135m of Zinc 681
(D) 50g / 135m of Snowdrop 670

NEEDLES

4mm (no 8) (US 6) needles

COLOUR BLOCK SCARF

SIZE
18cm x 200cm / 7in x 78¾in

TENSION
24 stitches and 22 rows to 10cm/4in
Measured over pattern using 4mm
(US 6) needles.

SCARF
Using 4mm (US 6) needles and yarn A cast
on 42 stitches.
Row 1: (RS) Knit.
Row 2: (WS) * Knit 1, slip 1 stitch purlwise,
repeat from * to last 2 stitches, knit 2.
Row 3: Knit.
Row 4: Knit 2, * slip 1 stitch purlwise, knit 1,
repeat from * to end.
These 4 rows form pattern.
Work in pattern until work measures
40cm/15¾in, ending with a WS row.
Break off yarn A and join in yarn B.
Work in pattern for a further
40cm/15¾in, ending with a WS row.
Break off yarn B and join in yarn C.
Work in pattern for a further 40cm/15¾in,
ending with a WS row.
Break off yarn C and join in yarn D.
Work in pattern for a further 40cm/15¾in,
ending with a WS row.
Break off yarn D and join in yarn A.
Work in pattern for a further 40cm/15¾in,
ending with a WS row.
Cast off.

MAKING UP
Press as described on the information page
(see page 140).
Make 40 tassels, spacing 20 evenly along each
short edge. Make each tassel by cutting
6 x 22cm/8¾in lengths of yarn A, group
together and fold in half, attach through the
cast on and cast off edges of the scarf from
front to back.

DESK TIDY

We all have those bits and pieces that need to be tidied away on a desk. So, this is a brilliant way to create a modern space, using a recycled tin can and colourful DK yarn. The cable design creates elasticity in the fabric so that the cover will stay nicely in place.

SKILL LEVEL: REQUIRES EXPERIENCE

YOU'LL NEED:

YARN
25g / 65m of Rowan Summerlite DK or any No.3 Light weight yarn (photographed in Summer 453, Coral Blush 467 & Lagoon 457)

NEEDLES
3.75mm (no 9) (US 5) needles

EXTRAS
Cable needle

DESK TIDY

SIZE

One size – will fit an average size tin can

TENSION

34 stitches and 34 rows to 10cm/4in
Measured over pattern using 3.75mm
(US 5) needles

SPECIAL ABBREVIATIONS

C6B – slip next 3 stitches onto a cable
needle and hold at back of work, knit next 3
stitches, knit 3 stitches from cable needle.

DESK TIDY

Using 3.75mm (US 5) needles cast on 79sts.
Next Row: (RS) Purl.
Row 1: (WS) Knit 1 * knit 1, purl 3, knit 1,
purl 6, repeat from * to last stitch, knit 1.
Row 2: (RS) Purl 1 * knit 6, purl 1, knit 1,
slip 1, knit 1, purl 1 repeat from * to last
stitch, purl 1.
Row 3: Knit 1 * knit 1, purl 3, knit 1, purl 6,
repeat from * to last stitch, knit 1.

Row 4: Purl 1 * C6B, purl 1, knit 1, slip 1, knit 1,
purl 1 repeat from * to last stitch, purl 1.
Row 5: Knit 1 * knit 1, purl 3, knit 1, purl 6,
repeat from * to last stitch, knit 1.
Row 6: Purl 1 * knit 6, purl 1, knit 1, slip 1,
knit 1, purl 1 repeat from * to last stitch,
purl 1.
Row 7: Knit 1 * knit 1, purl 3, knit 1, purl 6,
repeat from * to last stitch, knit 1.
Row 8: Purl 1 * knit 6, purl 1, knit 1, slip 1,
knit 1, purl 1 repeat from * to last stitch,
purl 1.
Row 9: Knit 1 * knit 1, purl 3, knit 1, purl 6,
repeat from * to last stitch, knit 1.
Rows 4 – 9 form pattern.
Repeat pattern 5 times more.
Next Row: (RS) Purl.
Cast off.

MAKING UP

Press as described on the information page
(see page 140).
Join side seams using mattress stitch.

HOT WATER BOTTLE COVER

Snuggle up in a chair with this modern hot water bottle cover. You can choose your favourite colour yarns and buttons to personalise your design, which also makes it the perfect gift. The ribbed collar gives you easy access to refill your hot water bottle and the button closure keeps everything neat and tidy.

SKILL LEVEL: SOME EXPERIENCE

YOU'LL NEED:

YARN
Rowan Baby Merino Silk DK or any No.3 light-weight yarn
(A) 35g / 95m of Pastel Green 705
(B) 45g / 122m of Frosty 702

NEEDLES
4mm (no 8) (US 6) needles
3.75mm (no 9) (US 5) needles
4 x 3.75mm (no 9) (US 5) double-pointed needles

EXTRAS
Stitch holders.
3 medium buttons.

HOT BOTTLE WATER COVER

SIZE
Finished size 19cm x 30cm / 7½in x 11¾in.

TENSION
22 stitches and 30 rows to 10cm/4in
Measured over stocking stitch using 4mm
(US 6) needles

STRIPE SEQUENCE
Rows 1 – 6: Yarn A
Rows 7 – 12: Yarn B

FRONT
Using 4mm (US 6) needles and
yarn A cast on 34 stitches.
Keeping stripe sequence correct
throughout continue as follows
carrying yarn up side of work;
Starting with a knit row work in
stocking stitch for 2 rows.
Next Row: Knit 2, make 1, knit to
last 2 stitches, make 1, knit 2. 36 stitches.
Next Row: Purl.
Repeat last 2 rows 3 times more. 42 stitches.
Work straight for a further 62 rows, ending
on row 12 of stripe repeat.
Next Row: (RS) Knit 2, slip 1, knit 1, pass
slipped stitch over, knit to last 4 stitches, knit
2 together, knit 2. 40 stitches.
Next Row: Purl.
Repeat last 2 rows 3 times more. 34 stitches
Next Row: (RS) Knit 2, slip 1, knit 1, pass
slipped stitch over, knit to last 4 stitches, knit
2 together, knit 2. 32 stitches.
Next Row: Purl 2, purl 2 together through
back loop, purl to last 4 stitches, purl 2
together, purl 2. 30 stitches.
Repeat last 2 rows 4 times more. 14 stitches.
Leave rem 22 stitches on a stitch holder.

BOTTOM BACK

Using 4mm (US 6) needles and yarn A cast on 34 stitches.

Keeping stripe sequence correct throughout, continue as follows carrying yarn up side of the work:

Starting with a knit row work in stocking stitch for 2 rows.

Next Row: Knit 2, make 1, knit to last 2 stitches, make 1, knit 2. 36 stitches.

Next Row: Purl.

Repeat last 2 rows 3 times more. 42 stitches. Work straight for a further 32 rows, ending on row 6 of stripe repeat.

Change to 3.75mm (US 5) needles and continue in yarn B only.

Next Row: (RS) Knit 2, * purl 2, knit 2 repeat from * to end.

Next Row: Purl 2, * knit 2, purl 2 repeat from * to end.

Repeat last 2 rows twice more.

Cast off in pattern.

TOP BACK

Using 3.75mm (US 5) needles and yarn B cast on 42 stitches.

Next Row: (RS) Knit 2, * purl 2, knit 2 repeat from * to end.

Next Row: Purl 2, * knit 2, purl 2 repeat from * to end.

Buttonhole Row: Pattern 8, knit 2 together, yarn over, pattern 10, knit 2 together, yarn over, pattern 10, knit 2 together, yarn over, pattern to end.

Next Row: Purl 2, * knit 2, purl 2 repeat from * to end.

Next Row: Knit 2, * purl 2, knit 2 repeat from * to end.

Next Row: Purl 2, * knit 2, purl 2 repeat from * to end.

Change to 4mm (US 6) needles and working in stripe sequence as set for front continue as follows:

Starting with a knit row work a further 24 rows, ending on row 12 of stripe repeat.

Next Row: (RS) Knit 2, slip 1, knit 1, pass slipped stitch over, knit to last 4 stitches, knit 2 together, knit 2. 40 stitches.

Next Row: Purl.

Repeat last 2 rows 3 times more. 34 stitches

Next Row: (RS) Knit 2, slip 1, knit 1, pass slipped stitch over, knit to last 4 stitches, knit 2 together, knit 2. 32 stitches.

Next Row: Purl 2, purl 2 together through back loop, purl to last 4 stitches, purl 2 together, purl 2. 30 stitches.

Repeat last 2 rows 4 times more. 14 stitches. Leave rem 22 stitches on a stitch holder.

MAKING UP

Press as described on the information page (see page 140).

Sew up all side seams with top back rib onto of bottom back rib, using mattress stitch.

Using 3.75mm (US 5) double pointed needles evenly space the 28 stitches left on stitch holders over 3 of the needles.

Rejoin yarn B.

Next Round: * Knit 2, purl 2 repeat from * to end.

Repeat last round until the collar measures 16cm/6¼in.

Cast off in pattern.

Attach buttons.

TABLET COVER

Protect your electronic tablet with this really useful cover. The thickness of the yarn offers great protection and makes it perfect for when you are on the move. Personalize by making this project in your favourite colour and adding a sturdy button.

SKILL LEVEL: SOME EXPERIENCE

YOU'LL NEED:

YARN
75g / 128m (100g / 170m)
of Rowan Handknit Cotton or any No.4
medium-weight yarn
(photographed in Thunder 335)

NEEDLES
4mm (no 8) (US 6) needles
2 x 4mm (no 8) (US 6) double
pointed needles

EXTRAS
Cable needle.
1 medium button.

TABLET COVER

SIZE

S(M)

S = Tablet size 16cm x 22cm / 6¼in x 8¾in.

M = Tablet size 20cm x 28cm / 7¾in x 11in.

TENSION

19 stitches and 28 rows to 10cm/4in
Measured over stocking stitch using 4mm
(US 6) needles

SPECIAL ABBREVIATIONS

C4B – slip next 2 stitches onto a cable
needle and hold at back of work, knit next
2 stitches, knit 2 stitches from cable needle.
C4F – slip next 2 stitches onto a cable
needle and hold at front of work, knit next
2 stitches, knit 2 stitches from cable needle.

BACK

Using 4mm (US 6) needles
cast on 30(38) stitches.
Starting with a purl row, work in stocking
stitch until work measures 22(28)cm/
8¾(11)in, ending with a WS row.

FRONT

Using 4mm (US 6) needles
cast on 30(38) stitches
Next Row: (WS) Purl.
Row 1: (RS) Purl 5(9), knit 6,
C4B, C4F, knit 6, purl 5(9).
Row 2: Knit 5(9), purl to last
5(9) stitches, knit 5(9).
Row 3: Purl 5(9), knit 4, C4B,
knit 4, C4F, knit 4, purl 5(9).
Row 4: Knit 5(9), purl to last
5(9) stitches, knit 5(9).
Row 5: Purl 5(9), knit 2, C4B,
knit 8, C4F, knit 2, purl 5(9).

Row 6: Knit 5(9), purl to last
5(9) stitches, knit 5(9).
Row 7: Purl 5(9), C4B, knit 12,C4F, purl 5(9).
Row 8: Knit 5(9), purl to last 5(9) stitches,
knit 5(9).
Rows 1 – 8 form pattern.
Work in pattern until work measures
22(28)cm/8¾(11)in, ending with a WS row.
Cast off.

MAKING UP

Press as described on the information page
(see page 140).
Join side and bottom seams using mattress
stitch.
Using 4mm (US 6) double-pointed needles
cast on 3 stitches.
Knit these 3 stitches, * slide these stitches to
other end of needle, do not turn, pulling the
yarn across the back of the knitted stitches knit
into the right most stitch, knit remaining stitches,
repeat from * until i-cord measures 10cm/4in.
Cast off.
Attach cast on and cast off edge of i-cord to
the middle top of the back piece.
Attach button.

LACE WRAP

This fanned lace design is really pretty and creates a lovely texture and feel to the project. Make your wrap as long as you wish and it will be a perfect companion to any outfit. I used a yarn from my stash that had a chained texture which made the wrap really lightweight to wear.

SKILL LEVEL: SOME EXPERIENCE

YOU'LL NEED:

YARN
264g / 712m of Rowan Panama or any
No.1 Super Fine weight yarn
(photographed in Orchid 304)

NEEDLES
4mm (no 8) (US 6) needles

LACE WRAP

SIZE

35cm x 168cm / 13¾in x 66¼in

TENSION

28 stitches and 25 rows to 10cm/4in
Measured over lace pattern using 4mm
(US 6) needles

WRAP

Using 4mm (US 6) needles cast on 98 stitches.
Work 4 rows in garter stitch.

Row 1: (RS) Knit.

Row 2: Knit 4, purl to last 4 stitches, knit 4.

Row 3: Knit 4, (knit 2 together) three times,
* (yarn forward, knit 1) six times, (knit 2
together) six times, repeat from * three
times more, (yarn forward, knit 1) six times,
(knit 2 together) three times, knit 4.

Row 4: Knit 4, purl to last 4 stitches, knit 4.

Row 5: Knit.

Row 6: Knit 4, purl to last 4 stitches, knit 4.

Row 7: Knit 4, (knit 2 together) three times,

* (yarn forward, knit 1) six times, (knit 2
together) six times, repeat from * three
times more, (yarn forward, knit 1) six times,
(knit 2 together) three times, knit 4.

Row 8: Knit 4, purl to last 4 stitches, knit 4.

Row 9: Knit.

Row 10: Knit 4, purl to last 4 stitches, knit 4.

Row 11: Knit 4, (knit 2 together) three
times, * (yarn forward, knit 1) six times, (knit
2 together) six times, repeat from * three
times more, (yarn forward, knit 1) six times,
(knit 2 together) three times, knit 4.

Row 12: Knit.

Rows 1 – 12 set pattern.

Work in pattern until work measures 165cm/
65in, ending on row 12 of pattern repeat.

Work 4 rows in garter stitch.

Cast off loosely.

MAKING UP

Press as described on the information page
(see page 140).

Key

☐	RS: knit / WS: purl
●	RS: purl / WS: knit
╱	RS: k2tog / WS: p2tog
○	yfwd
☐	Repeat

Row numbers (right side, odd): 11, 9, 7, 5, 3, 1

Column numbers (bottom): 44 43 42 41 40 39 38 37 36 35 34 33 32 31 30 29 28 27 26 25 24 23 22 21 20 19 18 17 16 15 14 13 12 11 10 9 8 7 6 5 4 3 2 1

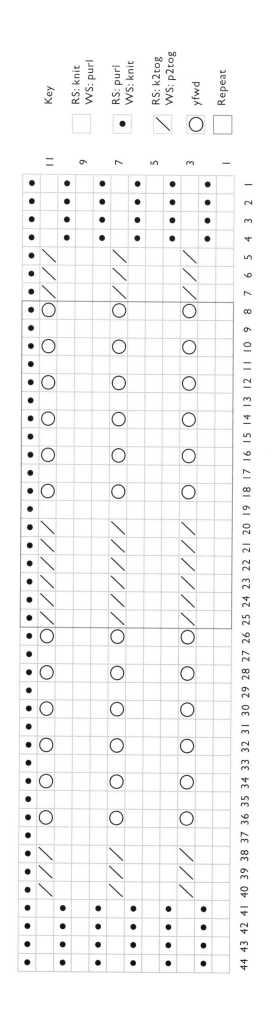

LAVENDER PILLOW

A lavender pillow is a really great idea to scent any drawers or wardrobes. It also makes a perfect gift for that special someone and can be filled with fresh lavender or dried lavender buds.

SKILL LEVEL: SOME EXPERIENCE

YOU'LL NEED:

YARN
Rowan Superfine Merino 4ply or any
No.1 Super Fine weight yarn
(A) 20g / 66m of Marble 269
(B) 8g / 26m of Polar 261

NEEDLES
3.25mm (no 10) (US 3) needles
2 x 3.25mm (no 10) (US 3) double-
pointed needles

EXTRAS
Stuffing.
Lavender – we used dried lavender.

LAVENDER PILLOW

SIZE
11cm x 12cm / 4¼in x 4¾in

TENSION
28 stitches and 36 rows to 10cm/4in
Measured over stocking stitch using
3.25mm (US 3) needles.

LAVENDER PILLOW
BACK
Using yarn A and 3.25mm (US 3) needles
cast on 31 stitches.
Starting with a knit row, work in stocking
stitch for 44 rows.
Cast off.
FRONT
Using yarn A and 3.25mm (US 3) needles
cast on 31 stitches.
Starting with a knit row, work in stocking
stitch for 10 rows.
Place chart.

Next Row: (RS) Knit 3, place row 1 of
chart, knit 3.
Next Row: (WS) Purl 3, place row 2 of
chart, purl 3.
Last 2 rows place the chart, continue as set
until all 22 rows of chart have been worked.
Work in stocking stitch until front matches
length of back.
Cast off.

MAKING UP
Press as described on the information page
(see page 140).
Using mattress stitch, join 3 of the 4 sides,
using mattress stitch. Stuff the pillow with
stuffing and lavender. Join last seam. Using
3.25mm (US 3) double pointed needles cast
on 3 stitches. Knit these 3 stitches, * slide
these stitches to other end of needle, do not
turn, pulling the yarn across the back of the
knitted stitches knit into the right most stitch.
Knit remaining stitches, repeat from * until
i-cord measures 10cm/4in.

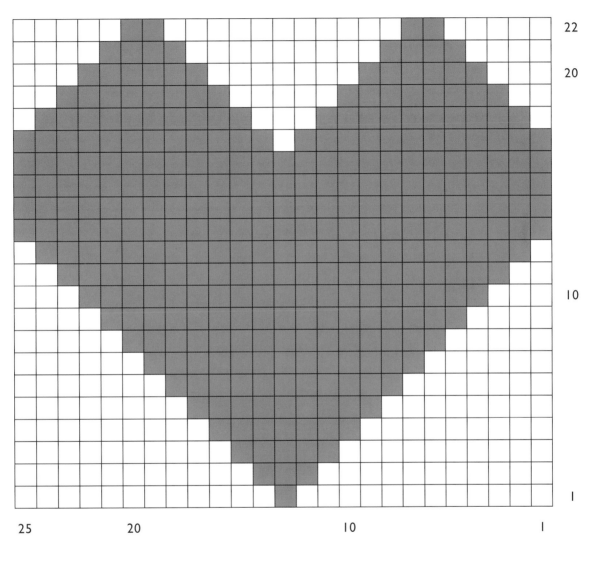

Key

☐ Yarn A

▨ Yarn B

MITRED CORNER CUSHION

This cushion was designed to enable you to use as many or as few colours from your stash as you wish. Customize the design to work within your chosen room's colour scheme and to add a nice textural focal piece.

SKILL LEVEL: SOME EXPERIENCE

YOU'LL NEED:

YARN
Rowan Handknit Cotton or any No.4
Medium weight yarn
(A) 35g / 60m of Forest 370
(B) 8g / 14m of Ecru 251
(C) 35g / 60m of North Sea 371
(D) 8g / 14m of Sea Foam 352
(E) 35g / 60m of Sunshine 354
(F) 8g / 14m of Gooseberry 219
(G) 35g / 60m of Slate 347
(H) 8g / 14m of Celery 309

NEEDLES
4mm (no 8) (US 6) needles

EXTRAS
Stitch marker.
Cushion pad 45cm x 45cm / 18in x 18in.
Two pieces of fabric for backing
measuring 50cm x 50cm / 20in x 20in
if making your own cushion cover or a
premade cushion cover measuring
45cm x 45cm / 18in x 18in.

MITRED CORNER CUSHION

SIZE

45cm x 45cm / 18in x 18in

TENSION

20 stitches and 40 rows to 10cm/4in
Measured over garter stitch using 4mm
(US 6) needles

CUSHION

Using yarn A and 4mm (US 6) needles cast
on 83 stitches.

Work 2 rows in garter stitch.

Next Row: (RS) Knit 39, knit 2 together,
place marker, knit 1, knit 2 together, knit to
end. 81 stitches.

Next Row: Knit.

Next Row: Knit to 2 stitches before marker,
knit 2 together, slip marker, knit 1, knit 2
together, knit to end. 79 stitches.

Next Row: Knit.

Repeat last 2 rows to 39 stitches.

Change to yarn B and continue
as set to 3 stitches.

Next Row: Knit 3 together.
Fasten off.

With RS facing using yarn C and 4mm
(US 6) needles pick up and knit 42 stitches
down left side of cast on edge of first square.
Cast on 41 stitches. 83 stitches.

Next Row: (WS) Knit.

Next Row: (RS) Knit 39, knit 2 together,
place marker, knit 1, knit 2 together, knit to
end. 81 stitches.

Next Row: Knit.

Next Row: Knit to 2 stitches before marker,
knit 2 together, slip marker, knit 1, knit 2
together, knit to end. 79 stitches.

Next Row: Knit.

Repeat last 2 rows to 39 stitches.

Change to yarn D and continue as set to 3
stitches.

Next Row: Knit 3 together.
Fasten off.

With RS facing using yarn E and 4mm (US 6) needles pick up and knit 41 stitches along cast on edge of second square. Cast on 42 stitches. 83 stitches.

Next Row: (WS) Knit.

Next Row: (RS) Knit 39, knit 2 together, place marker, knit 1, knit 2 together, knit to end. 81 stitches.

Next Row: Knit.

Next Row: Knit to 2 stitches before marker, knit 2 together, slip marker, knit 1, knit 2 together, knit to end. 79 stitches.

Next Row: Knit.

Repeat last 2 rows to 39 stitches.

Change to yarn F and continue to 3 stitches.

Next Row: Knit 3 together.

Fasten off.

With RS facing using yarn G and 4mm (US 6) needles pick up and knit 42 stitches along cast on edge of third square made and 41 stitches along remaining side of first square.

Next Row: (WS) Knit.

Next Row: (RS) Knit 39, knit 2 together, place marker, knit 1, knit 2 together, knit to end. 81 stitches.

Next Row: Knit.

Next Row: Knit to 2 stitches before marker, knit 2 together, slip marker, knit 1, knit 2 together, knit to end. 79 stitches.

Next Row: Knit.

Repeat last 2 rows to 39 stitches.

Change to yarn H and continue as set to 3 stitches.

Next Row: Knit 3 together.

Fasten off.

MAKING UP

Press as described on the information page (see page 140).

We chose to make our own cushion cover by placing the wrong sides of fabric together, using a 2.5cm seam allowance sew 3 of the 4 sides together. Turn right way out and press open seam 2.5cm inwards. Hand stitch knitted cover to one of the pieces. Stitch final seam encasing the cushion pad.

TEXTURED BABY BEANIE

This baby beanie is designed for a new born baby, up until around the age of six months. The moss stitch texture is a great way to add something a little more modern to a baby's wardrobe and is great when made in lots of different colours. The design matches perfectly with the baby booties in this book (see page 36).

SKILL LEVEL: EASY

YOU'LL NEED:

YARN
25g / 68m of Rowan Baby Merino Silk DK or
any No.3 light-weight yarn
(photographed in Dawn 672)

NEEDLES
3.5mm (no 9/10) (US 4) needles
4mm (no 8) (US 6) needles

EXTRAS
Pompom (optional)

TEXTURED BABY BEANIE

SIZE

0 – 6 months

TENSION

26sts and 44 rows to 10cm/4in
Measured over moss st pattern
using 4mm (US 6) needles.

HAT

Using 3.5mm (US 4) needles cast on
90 stitches.
Row 1: (RS) * Knit 1, purl 1 repeat from * to end.
Repeat last row until work measures
5cm/2in, ending with a wrong side row.
Change to 4mm (US 6) needles.
Row 1: (RS) * Knit 1, purl 1 repeat from * to end.
Row 2: * Purl 1, knit 1 repeat from * to end.
Last 2 rows set moss stitch pattern.
Work in moss stitch pattern until work
measures 11cm/4¼in from cast-on edge.

SHAPE CROWN

Next Row: * Pattern 7 stitches, slip 1 stitch,
knit 2 together, pass slipped stitch over, rep
from * to end. 81 stitches.
Pattern 1 row.
Next Row: * Pattern 6 stitches, slip 1 stitch,
knit 2 together, pass slipped stitch over, rep
from * to end. 72 stitches.
Pattern 1 row.
Next Row: * Pattern 5 stitches, slip 1 stitch,
knit 2 together, pass slipped stitch over, rep
from * to end. 63 stitches.
Pattern 1 row.
Next Row: * Pattern 4 stitches, slip 1 stitch,
knit 2 together, pass slipped stitch over, rep
from * to end. 54 stitches.
Pattern 1 row.
Next Row: * Pattern 3 stitches, slip 1 stitch,
knit 2 together, pass slipped stitch over, rep
from * to end. 45 stitches.
Pattern 1 row.

Next Row: * Pattern 2 stitches, slip 1 stitch, knit 2 together, pass slipped stitch over, rep from * to end. 36 stitches.

Pattern 1 row.

Next Row: Knit 2 together to end. 18 stitches.

Next Row: Purl 1, * Purl 2 together repeat from * to end. 9 stitches.

Cut yarn leaving a length long enough to sew up.

MAKING UP

Press as described on the information page (see page 140).

Thread yarn through remaining stitches and join side seams using mattress stitch (see page 134).

Attach pompom if desired.

For matching booties, see page 36.

BASKET

Storage for my yarn while working on a project is always something I seem to lack so this basket is a great way of keeping your project's yarn all together and allows you to easily knit while keeping the yarn within the basket. Of course, this could also be used to store a whole manner of other items too!

SKILL LEVEL: SOME EXPERIENCE

YOU'LL NEED:

YARN
250g / 288m of Rowan Cocoon or any
No.5 Bulky weight yarn
(photographed in Dove 849)

NEEDLES
10mm (no 000) (US 15) circular needles
60cm in length

BASKET

SIZE

30cm / 11¾in diameter and 18cm / 7in high

TENSION

10 stitches and 15 rows to 10cm/4in
Measured over moss stitch using 10mm
(US 15) needles and holding yarn double
throughout.

BASE

Using 10mm (US 15) needles and holding
yarn double cast on 10sts.
Row 1: (RS) *Knit 1, purl 1 repeat from * to end.
Row 2: *Purl 1, knit 1 repeat from * to end.
Last 2 rows set moss stitch, keeping moss
stitch pattern correct throughout taking
increases into pattern.
Inc 1st at each end of every following row to
30sts.
Work 10 rows in pattern.

Dec 1 st at each end of every following
row to 10sts.
Work 2 rows in pattern.
Cast off.

SIDES

With RS facing, using 10mm (US 15) needles
and holding yarn double pick up and knit
80sts around the side edges of base.
Round 1: * Purl 1, knit 1 repeat from
* to end of round.
Round 2: * Knit 1, purl 1 to end of round.
Last 2 rows set moss stitch pattern.
Rep last 2 rows until work measures
18cm/7in.
Cast off in pattern.

MAKING UP

Press as described on the information page
(see page 140).

MUG HUGS

Who doesn't love having a warm drink stay warm for even longer? Now you can, by making your own mug hugs which wrap perfectly around a standard mug and can be simply adjusted for larger mugs by making a slightly longer strap.

SKILL LEVEL: EASY

YOU'LL NEED:

YARN
Rowan Cocoon or any No.5 Bulky
weight yarn
(A) 20g / 23m of Misty Rose 851
(B) 15g / 18m of Scree 803

NEEDLES
10mm (no 000) (US 15) needles

EXTRAS
12mm Clear Snap fasteners – you will
need 2 pairs per mug hug.

MUG HUGS

SIZE
One size

TENSION
10.5 stitches and 12 rows to 10cm/4in
Measured over stocking stitch using 10mm
(US 15) needles holding yarn double
throughout.

MUG HUGS
MAIN SECTION
Using yarn A and 10mm (US 15)
needles cast on 15 stitches.
Work in garter stitch for 5 rows.
Change to yarn B.
Next Row: (WS) Knit.
Next Row: Purl.
Rep last 2 rows 3 times more.
Next Row: Knit.
Cast off knitwise.

BACK SECTION
Using yarn A and 10mm
(US 15) needles cast on 17 stitches.
Work in garter stitch for 4 rows.
Cast off knitwise.

MAKING UP
Press as described on the information page
(see page 140).
Place your main section around your chosen
mug, using pins mark where to stitch your
snap fasteners on both sections so that
the back section fits through the handle
comfortably. Attach your snap fasteners to
either side of the main section and on the
ends of the back section.

SIMPLE BEANIE

A simple beanie can be found in most wardrobes and with wear and tear it's always lovely to have a fresh hat to wear each winter. I paired my simple design with a gorgeous faux fur pompom but, of course, you could make your own pompom using a pompom maker and some more stash yarn.

SKILL LEVEL: EASY

YOU'LL NEED:

YARN
70g / 80m of Rowan Cocoon or any No.5
Bulky weight yarn
(photographed in Frost 806)

NEEDLES
6.5mm (no 3) (US 10.5) needles
7mm (no 2) (US 10.5/11) needles

EXTRAS
Pompom (we used a Rowan faux fur pompom)

SIMPLE BEANIE

SIZE

To fit an average size adult woman's head

TENSION

14 stitches and 16 rows to 10cm/4in
Measured over stocking stitch using 7mm
(US 10.5/11) needles.

BEANIE

Using 6.5mm (US 10.5) needles cast on 72 stitches.
Row 1: (RS) * Knit 1, purl 1, repeat from * to end.
Last row sets rib pattern.
Work in rib for 7 rows more.
Change to 7mm (US 10.5/11) needles.
Starting with a knit row, work in stocking
stitch until work measures 17cm / 6¾in,
ending with a wrong side row.

SHAPE CROWN

Next Row: (RS) * Knit 4, knit 2 together
repeat from * to end. 60 stitches.
Next Row: Purl.

Next Row: * Knit 3, knit 2 together
repeat from * to end. 48 stitches.
Next Row: Purl.
Next Row: * Knit 2, knit 2 together
repeat from * to end. 36 stitches.
Next Row: Purl.
Next Row: * Knit 1, knit 2 together
repeat from * to end. 24 stitches.
Next Row: Purl.
Next Row: * Knit 2 together
repeat from * to end. 12 stitches.
Next Row: * Purl 2 together
repeat from * to end. 6 stitches.

MAKING UP

Press as described on the information page
(see page 140).
Thread yarn through remaining stitches
and sew up seam using mattress stitch
(see page 134).
Attach pompom if desired.

BABY STRIPED BEANIE

This design, created in super soft cotton, is the perfect lightweight beanie for a little one. While keeping the cold out, it also allows for heat to be regulated, without making baby too hot – which is perfect for a new born. Personalize your design by using different colours of your choice, or keep it neutral with a really soft colour palette.

SKILL LEVEL: EASY

YOU'LL NEED:

YARN
Rowan Summerlite DK or any No.3
light-weight yarn
(A) – 13g / 34m of Mushroom 454
(B) – 10g / 26m of White 465

NEEDLES
3.25mm (no 10) (US 3) needles
4mm (no 8) (US 6) needles

BABY STRIPED BEANIE

SIZE
0 – 6 months

TENSION
22 sts and 30 rows to 10cm/4in
Measured over stocking stitch
using 4mm (US 6) needles.

HAT
Using 3.25mm (US 3) needles
and yarn A cast on 78 stitches.
Row 1: (RS) Knit 2, * purl 2, knit 2
repeat from * to end.
Row 2: Purl 2, * knit 2, purl 2
repeat from * to end.
Repeat last 2 rows twice more.
Stripe sequence:
Rows 1 – 6: Yarn B
Rows 7 – 12: Yarn A

Change to 4mm (US 6) needles and yarn B.
Starting with a knit row work in stocking
stitch and keeping stripe sequence correct
until work measures 10cm/4in, ending with
a wrong side row.

SHAPE CROWN
Next Row: (RS) *Knit 11, knit 2 together
repeat from * to end. 72 stitches.
Next Row: Purl.
Next Row: (RS) *Knit 10, knit 2 together
repeat from * to end. 66 stitches.
Next Row: Purl.
Next Row: (RS) *Knit 9, knit 2 together
repeat from * to end. 60 stitches.
Next Row: Purl.
Next Row: (RS) *Knit 8, knit 2 together
repeat from * to end. 54 stitches.
Next Row: Purl.
Next Row: (RS) *Knit 7, knit 2 together
repeat from * to end. 48 stitches.
Next Row: Purl.

Next Row: Knit 2 together to end. 24 stitches.
Next Row: Purl 2 together to end. 12 stitches.
Cut yarn, leaving enough length to sew up hat.

MAKING UP

Press as described on the information page
(see page 140).
Thread yarn through remaining stitches
and join seam using mattress stitch (see
page 134).

STRIPED BLANKET

This blanket has been designed to be a really fun way to bring colour into your child's room. The yarn has been doubled to create a fabric that is thicker and makes the blanket sturdier. Great for being used all over the house, or even outside on a picnic.

SKILL LEVEL: EASY

YOU'LL NEED:

YARN
Rowan Summerlite DK or any No.3 Light weight yarn
(A) 85g / 221m of Fuchsia 455
(B) 85g / 221m of Summer 453
(C) 85g / 221m of Linen 460
(D) 85g / 221m of Silvery Blue 468
(E) 85g / 221m of Favourite Denims 469
(F) 85g / 221m of Sailor Blue 470

NEEDLES
6mm (no 4) (US 10) needles

STRIPED BLANKET

SIZE

75cm x 100cm / 29½in x 39¼in

TENSION

14 stitches and 19 rows to 10cm/4in
Measured over garter stitch using 6mm
(US 10) needles and yarn held double
throughout.

BLANKET

Using 6mm (US 10) needles and 2 strands of
yarn A, cast on 105 stitches.
Work in garter stitch until work measures
14cm/5½in, ending with a wrong side row.
Change to yarn B.
Work in garter stitch for a further
14cm/5½in, ending with a wrong side row.
Change to yarn C.
Work in garter stitch for a further
14cm/5½in, ending with a wrong side row.

Change to yarn D.
Work in garter stitch for a further
14cm/5½in, ending with a wrong side row.
Change to yarn E.
Work in garter stitch for a further
14cm/5½in, ending with a wrong side row.
Change to yarn F.
Work in garter stitch for a further
14cm/5½in, ending with a wrong side row.
Cast off.

MAKING UP

Press as described on the information page
(see page 140).

STRIPED SCARF

Every stash probably has some black yarn sitting there so what better way to use it than as a contrast colour in a monochrome design. This pattern contains lots of colour changes which enables you to use up as many of your stash yarns as possible.

SKILL LEVEL: SOME EXPERIENCE

YOU'LL NEED:

YARN
Rowan Kid Classic or any No.4 Light
weight yarn
(A) 100g / 280m of Cement 890
(B) 70g / 196m of Drought 876
(C) 100g / 280m of Smoke 831

NEEDLES
4.5mm (no 7) (US 7) needles

STRIPED SCARF

SIZE

35cm wide x 158cm long / 13¾in wide x 62¼in long.

TENSION

20sts and 38rows to 10cm/4in
Measured over garter stitch using 4.5mm (US 7) needles.

SCARF

Using 4.5mm (US 7) needles
and yarn A cast on 70sts.
Work 2 rows in garter stitch.
Next Row: (RS) Knit 2, make 1, knit to last 4 stitches, knit 2 together, knit 2. 70 stitches.
Next Row: Knit.
Working shaping as set above, repeat last 2 rows and working in garter stitch throughout continue following stripe sequence below:
Rows 1 – 14: Yarn A
Rows 15 – 16: Yarn B

Rows 17 – 18: Yarn A
Rows 19 – 20: Yarn B
Rows 21 – 26: Yarn A
Rows 27 – 34: Yarn C
Rows 35 – 40: Yarn A
Rows 41 – 42: Yarn B
Rows 43 – 44: Yarn A
Rows 45 – 46: Yarn C
Rows 47 – 54: Yarn B
Rows 55 – 60: Yarn C
Rows 61 – 74: Yarn B
Rows 75 – 78: Yarn C
Rows 79 – 86: Yarn A
Rows 87 – 90: Yarn B
Rows 91 – 96: Yarn A
Rows 97 – 110: Yarn B
Rows 111- 134: Yarn A
Rows 135 – 142: Yarn C
Rows 143 – 150: Yarn A
Rows 151 – 176: Yarn C
Rows 177 – 186: Yarn A
Rows 187 – 196: Yarn B

Rows 197 – 220: Yarn C
Rows 221 – 246: Yarn A
Rows 247 – 270: Yarn B
Rows 271 – 280: Yarn A
Rows 281 – 282: Yarn B
Rows 283 – 284: Yarn A
Rows 285 – 286: Yarn C
Rows 287 – 288: Yarn A
Rows 289 – 290: Yarn C
Rows 291 – 300: Yarn A
Rows 301 – 330: Yarn C
Rows 331 – 346: Yarn A
Rows 347 – 368: Yarn B
Rows 369 – 390: Yarn A
Rows 391 – 420: Yarn C
Rows 421 – 440: Yarn B
Rows 441 – 446: Yarn C
Rows 447 – 450: Yarn B
Rows 451 – 456: Yarn C
Rows 457 – 470: Yarn A

Rows 471 – 484: Yarn C
Rows 485 – 490: Yarn B
Rows 491 – 494: Yarn C
Rows 495 – 502: Yarn A
Rows 503 – 510: Yarn C
Rows 511 – 514: Yarn B
Rows 515 – 518: Yarn C
Rows 519 – 522: Yarn A
Work in garter stitch for 2 rows without shaping in yarn C.
Cast off.

MAKING UP
Press as described on the information page (see page 140).

TEA COSY

There is nothing better than setting the table for tea and cake and being able to show off a statement tea cosy. This cosy is just that, and contains a really simple yet effective Fair Isle motif. Finish with a knitted pompom design and leave your guests wondering just how it was made!

SKILL LEVEL: REQUIRES EXPERIENCE

YOU'LL NEED:

YARN
Rowan Handknit Cotton or any No.4
light-weight yarn
(A) 30g / 51m of Ice Water 239
(B) 35g / 60m of Ecru 251
(C) 10g / 17m of Linen 205

NEEDLES
4mm (no 8) (US 6) needles

EXTRAS
Stitch holders.

TEA COSY

SIZE
To fit a small to medium tea pot

TENSION
20 stitches and 28 rows to 10cm/4in
Measured over stocking stitch using 4mm
(US 6) needles

TEA COSY – MAKE TWO
(front and back both alike)
Using 4mm (US 6) needles and yarn A
cast on 48 stitches
Row 1: (RS) * Knit 2, purl 2 repeat
from * to end.
Last row sets rib pattern.
Work in rib pattern for a further 7 rows.
** Change to yarn B.
Starting with a knit row, work
in stocking stitch for 4 rows.
Change to yarn A.
Work in stocking stich for 2 rows.

Place chart using the Fair Isle technique
described, and work the chart entirely in
stocking stitch, beginning with a right-side row.
Next Row: (RS) Work row 1 of chart 8
times across the row.
Next Row: (WS) Work row 2 of chart 8
times across the row.
Last 2 rows set chart placement.
Continue until all 7 rows of chart are complete.
Continue in yarn A only, work 1 row.
Repeat from ** once more.
Change to yarn B.
Next Row: (RS) * Knit 2 together, knit 6
repeat from * to end. 42 stitches.
Next Row: Purl.
Next Row: Knit.
Next Row: * Purl 5, purl 2 together
repeat from * to end. 36 stitches.
Change to yarn A.
Next Row: Knit.
Next Row: Purl.
Next Row: * Knit 4, knit 2 together

repeat from * to end. 30 stitches.

Next Row: Purl.

Next Row: * Knit 2 together,
knit 3 repeat from * to end. 24 stitches.

Next Row: Purl.

Next Row: * Knit 2 together,
knit 2 repeat from * to end. 18 stitches.

Next Row: Purl.

Next Row: * Knit 2 together,
knit 1 repeat from * to end. 12 stitches.
Leave rem stitches on a stitch holder.
Break yarn leaving a long enough length
to sew up.

MAKING UP

Press as described on the information page
(see page 140).
Sew the side seams of tea cosy leaving a gap
each side big enough for the handle and spout.
Using a tail end of yarn A, pull through all
stitches left on stitch holders, pull tight to fasten.

Pompom

Using 4mm needles and yarn B cast on
20 stitches.

Row 1: (RS) Cast off 16 stitches, knit 4.
4 stitches.

Row 2: Knit 4, turn, cast on 16 stitches.
20 stitches.
Repeat last 2 rows 19 times more then
row 1 once more.
Cast off.
Starting at cast on edge, roll up strip to make
pompom and use tail yarn to sew up and
secure as you go.
Attach to top of tea cosy.

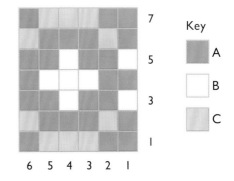

TEXTURED BAG

This chunky knitted bag is perfect for taking to the shops and filling with your new yarn purchases. It is lightweight but still has structure and holds its shape really well. You could always go one step further and make a fabric lining for it if you plan to carry heavier items.

SKILL LEVEL: SOME EXPERIENCE

YOU'LL NEED:

YARN
700g / 560m of Rowan Big Wool or any
No.6 Super Bulky weight yarn
(photographed in Pantomime 79)

NEEDLES
10mm (no 0) (US 15) needles

EXTRAS
2 × bag handles.
8 × stitch markers.

TEXTURED BAG

SIZE
One size

TENSION
10 stitches and 11 rows to 10cm/4in
Measured over patter using 10mm
(US 15) needles

SIDES – MAKE 4
BASE
Using 10mm (US 15) needles cast on 2 stitches.
Next Row: Knit into the front and back of both stitches. 4 stitches.
Next Row: Knit into the front and back of next stitch, working in purl 1, knit 1, moss stitch work to last stitch, knitting in the front and back of last stitch. 6 stitches.
Working increases as set above and keeping moss stitch pattern correct throughout, taking increases into pattern.
Increase one stitch at each end of every row to 46 stitches.
Place a stitch marker at each end of last row.

SIDE PANEL
Row 1: Pattern to end.
Row 2: Pattern to end.
Row 3: * Purl 1, with yarn at front of work slip next stitch knitwise repeat from *to last stitch, knit 1.
Row 4: Pattern to end.
Repeat rows 3 and 4, 19 times more.
Work 3 rows in moss stitch.
Cast off.

MAKING UP
Press as described on the information page (see page 140).
Join each panel; starting at the cast on edge, join each panel using mattress stitch, using markers as a guide to match up corners, repeat for remaining 3 seams.
Attach 2 handles of your choice approximately on opposites sides 5cm/2in down from the cast on edge on the wrong side of your bag.

TEXTURED BEANIE

If you are looking for a beanie that carries some texture but don't want to take on the cable beanie, then this is a great alternative. The simple moss stitch paired with the ribbed brim work really well together. Here I have added a pompom made from yarn but, of course, you could also use a faux fur pompom too!

SKILL LEVEL: EASY

YOU'LL NEED:

YARN
50g / 140m of Rowan Kid Classic or any
No.4 Medium weight yarn
(photographed in Drought 876)

NEEDLES
4.5mm (no 7) (US 7) needles
5mm (no 6) (US 8) needles

EXTRAS
Pompom (optional).

TEXTURED BEANIE

SIZE
To fit an adult woman's head

TENSION
19sts and 32 rows to 10cm/4in
Measured over moss st pattern using 5mm (US 8) needles.

HAT
Using 4.5mm (US 7) needles cast on 90 stitches.

Row 1: * Knit 1, purl 1 repeat from * to end.
Repeat last row until work measures 5cm/2in, ending with a wrong side row.
Change to 5mm (US 8) needles.

Row 1: (RS) * Purl 1, knit 1 repeat from * to end.

Row 2: * Knit 1, purl 1 repeat from * to end.
Last 2 rows set moss stitch pattern.
Work in moss stitch pattern until work measures 18cm/7in, ending with a wrong side row.

SHAPE CROWN
Next Row: * Pattern 7 stitches, slip 1, pattern 2 together, pass slipped stitch over repeat from * to end. 72 stitches.
Next Row: Pattern to end.
Next Row: * Pattern 5 stitches, slip 1, pattern 2 together, pass slipped stitch over repeat from * to end. 54 stitches.
Next Row: Pattern to end.
Next Row: * Pattern 3 stitches, slip 1, pattern 2 together, pass slipped stitch over repeat from * to end. 36 stitches
Next Row: Pattern to end.
Next Row: * Pattern 1 stitch, slip 1, pattern 2 together, pass slipped stitch over repeat from * to end. 18 stitches
Next Row: Pattern to end.
Next Row: Knit 2 together to end. 9 stitches.
Cut yarn, leaving enough length to sew up hat.

MAKING UP

Press as described on the information page
(see page 140).
Thread yarn through remaining stitches and
sew up seam using mattress stitch.
Attach pompom if desired.

TEXTURED CUSHION

This cushion uses chunky yarn to create a firm moss stitch texture that works perfectly with a fabric backing. Great for styling your living room and snuggling up on the sofa with. If you don't want to make a fabric back, you could just knit two fronts and simply mattress stitch the seams together.

SKILL LEVEL: EASY

YOU'LL NEED:

YARN
220g / 187m Rowan Big Wool or any
No.6 Super Bulky weight yarn
(photographed in Concrete 061)

NEEDLES
10mm (no 000) (US 15) needles

EXTRAS
Cushion Pad 50cm x 50cm / 20in x 20in.
Two pieces of fabric for backing
measuring 55cm x 55cm / 21¾in x
21¾in if making your own cushion cover
or a premade cushion cover measuring
50cm x 50cm / 20in x 20in.

TEXTURED CUSHION

SIZE

50cm x 50cm / 20in x 20in

TENSION

10 stitches and 18 rows to 10cm/4in
Measured over moss stitch using 10mm
(US 15) needles

CUSHION

Using 10mm (US 15) needles
cast on 51 stitches.
Row 1: (RS) Knit 1, * purl 1,
knit 1 repeat from * to end.
Repeat last row until work measures
50cm/20in, ending with a wrong side row.
Cast off in pattern.

MAKING UP

Press as described on the information page
(see page 140).
We chose to make our own cushion cover
by placing the wrong sides of fabric together,
using a 2.5cm/1in seam allowance sew 3 of
the 4 sides together.
Turn right way out and press open seam
2.5cm/1in inwards. Hand stitch knitted
cover to one of the pieces. Stitch final seam
encasing the cushion pad.

TEXTURED SNOOD

By combining lace and cable techniques this snood creates a really eye-catching texture. It works perfectly with heavier weight yarns that you may have in your stash and can look great worn in different ways.

SKILL LEVEL: SOME EXPERIENCE

YOU'LL NEED:

YARN
190g / 152m of Rowan Big Wool or any
No.6 Super Bulky weight yarn
(photographed in Prize 064)

NEEDLES
10mm (no 000) (US 15) needles

TEXTURED SNOOD

SIZE
22cm x 120cm / 8¾in x 47¼in

TENSION
11sts and 10 rows to 10cm/4in
Measured over pattern using 10mm
(US 15) needles

SNOOD
Using 10mm (US 15) needles cast on
24 stitches.

Row 1: (WS) Slip 1 stitch knitwise with
yarn in front, purl 3, * yarn over, purl 2
repeat from * to end. 34 stitches.

Row 2: (RS) Slip 1 stitch purlwise with
yarn at back, knit 1 * drop yarn over from
previous row, knit second stitch through
the back loop, do not slip this stitch off the
needle, knit the first stitch on needle, slip
both stitches off needle repeat from * to
last 2 stitches, knit 2. 24 stitches.
Last 2 rows set pattern.

Repeat last 2 rows until work measures
120cm/47¼in, ending on Row 2 of pattern.
Cast off loosely.

MAKING UP
Press as described on the information page
(see page 140).
Join cast on and cast off edges using
mattress stitch.

WRIST WARMERS

These wrist warmers are great for those colder days, and make a brilliant gift for those people who have everything. If you have any lovely soft DK yarn in your stash then these are the perfect project.

SKILL LEVEL: SOME EXPERIENCE

YOU'LL NEED:

YARN
52g / 130m of Rowan Alpaca Soft DK or any No.3 Light weight yarn
(photographed in Rainy Day 210)

NEEDLES
3.25mm (no 10) (US 3) needles
4mm (no 8) (US 6) needles

WRIST WARMERS

SIZE

To fit average sized adult woman's hand

TENSION

22sts and 30rows to 10cm/4in
Measured over stocking stitch using 4mm
(US 6) needles

WRISTWARMERS – MAKE 2

Using 3.25mm (US 3) needles
cast on 42 stitches.
Row 1: (RS) * Knit 2, purl 2,
repeat from * to last 2 stitches, knit 2.
Row 2: Purl 2, * knit 2, purl 2,
repeat from * to end.
Last 2 rows set pattern.
Work in pattern until work measures
5cm/2in, ending with a wrong side row.
Change to 4mm (US 6) needles.
Starting with a knit row work 24
rows in stocking stitch.

SHAPE THUMB

Next Row: Knit 23, turn.
Next Row: Cast on 7 stitches, purl 11, turn.
Next Row: Cast on 7 stitches, knit 18.
Work on these 18sts for 4cm/1½in,
ending with a wrong side row.
Change to 3.25mm (US 3) needles.
Next Row: Knit 2, * purl 2, knit 2,
repeat from * to end.
Next Row: Purl 2, * knit 2,
purl 2, repeat from * to end.
Repeat last row 2 rows once more.
Cast off.
Sew thumb seam.
With right side facing, pick up 14 stitches
from base of thumb, knit to end. 52 stitches.
Starting with a purl row, cont in stocking
stitch until work measures 17cm/6¾in,
increasing 2 stitches across last row, ending
with a wrong side row. 54 stitches.
Change to 3.25mm (US 3) needles.

Row 1: (RS) * Knit 2, purl 2,
repeat from * to last 2 stitches, knit 2.
Row 2: Purl 2, * knit 2, purl 2,
repeat from * to end.
Repeat last row 2 rows once more.
Cast off.

MAKING UP

Press as described on the information page
(see page 140).
Sew up side seam.

FINISHING TECHNIQUES

Finishing techniques

MATTRESS STITCH

This technique produces an almost invisible seam that is slightly stiffer and bulkier than a grafted seam, but it is a simple technique to work. As mattress stitch is worked row by row on the right side, it is perfect for joining colour work: a touch of magic when piecing stripes together. The other advantage to this technique is that if the yarn you have knitted with has too loose a twist or is too frail to sew up with, you can use another yarn of a similar colour and it won't show. Do not knot one end of the yarn. Instead, leave a tail and when you have completed the seam, sew in the tails at both ends. The sewing yarn in these illustrations is a contrast colour to help you see how the stitches are made.

SEWING STOCKING STITCHES TO STITCHES

This is most commonly used for joining shoulder seams. Right-sides up, lay the two pieces to be joined side by side. Thread a tapestry needle with a long length of yarn.

1 From the back, bring the tapestry needle up through the first stitch in the lower piece of knitted fabric.

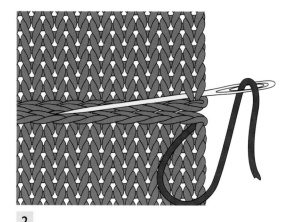

2 Take the needle under both loops of the same stitch on the other piece, so that it emerges between the first and second stitches.

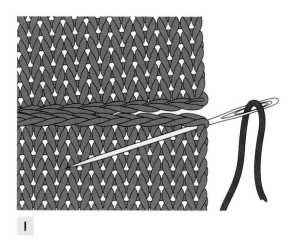

3 Go back into the lower piece where the needle first came out and take it under one loop, so that it emerges between the first and second stitches.

4 Take the needle under both loops of the second stitch on the upper piece, then under both loops of the second stitch on the lower piece. Continue in this way. When you have sewn about 5cm (2in) of the seam, gently pull the stitches up to close the seam.

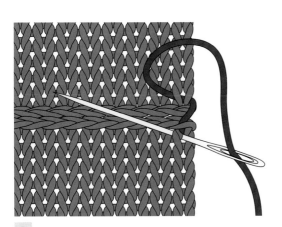

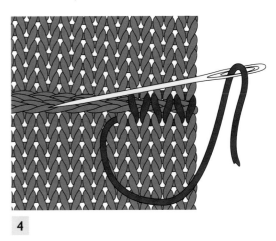

SEWING STOCKING STITCH ROW ENDS TO ROW ENDS

This technique will usually be used when sewing up side seams. Here it is shown worked half a stitch in from the edges, but you can work a whole stitch in if you prefer (or if your edge stitches tend to be baggy). Right-sides up, lay the two pieces to be joined side by side. Thread a tapestry needle with a long length of yarn.

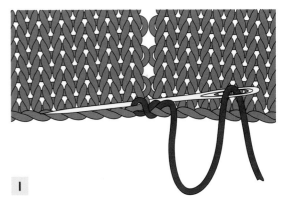

1 To start the seam, bring the needle from the back of the right-hand piece through the centre of the first stitch of the first row. Take it across to the other piece and, from the back bring it through the first stitch. Take it back to the first piece and, again from the back, bring it through where it first came through. Finally take the needle through the back of the first stitch on the left-hand piece and pull tight the figure-of-eight you have made.

2 Take the needle across to the right hand piece and, from the front, take it through the middle of the first stitch and under the bar of yarn that divides that stitch from the one above. (If the knitted fabrics are both all one colour, and so precise matching is not important, you can take the needle under two stitch bars at a time.)

3 Take the needle across to the left-hand piece and, from the front, take it through the middle of the first stitch and under one (or two) bars. Continue up the seam, zigzagging between the two pieces, picking up the same number of stitch bars on either side. When you have sewn about 5cm (2in) of the seam, gently pull the stitches up to close the seam and then continue.

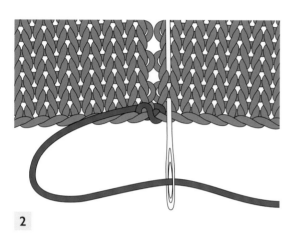

2

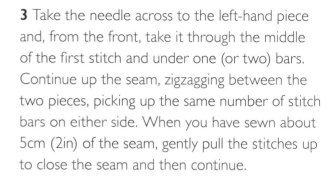

3

GRAFTING

Both pieces of knitting must have the same number of stitches. Work from right to left across the knitting, slipping the stitches off the needles one at a time once the tapestry needle has gone through them. Thread a tapestry needle with a long length of the project yarn (a contrast colour yarn has been used below to help you understand the technique).

1 Lay the pieces right-sides up on a flat surface with the needles together. From back to front, bring the tapestry needle through the first stitch of the lower piece and then through the first stitch of the upper piece. Take the needle through the front of the first stitch of the lower piece, then from the back, through the second stitch of the lower piece.

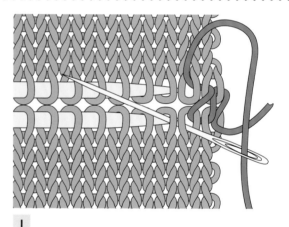

1

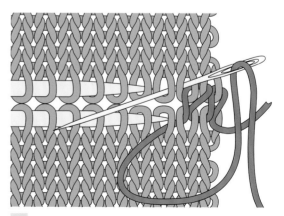

2

Go through the front of the first stitch on the upper piece and then through the back of the second stitch on the same piece.

2 Continue in this pattern across the row, taking the tapestry needle through the back and later the front of each stitch in turn.

3 Gently pull the sewn stitches as you work them so that they have the same tension (gauge) as the rest of the fabric.

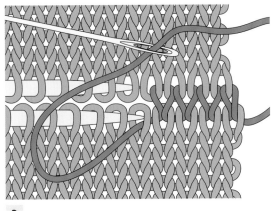

. . . .

PICKING UP STITCHES

How many of you have followed pattern instructions that say, 'Pick up and knit 46 stitches along left side of neck', and when you have 46 stitches on your needles you are still 4cm (1½in) from the end of the neck? Usually this is because you. are trying very hard to eliminate any holes and have picked up too many stitches in some areas. It's not a bad thing to have too many stitches, as long as you keep a note of how many extra there are and decrease to the right number on the first row of rib. Also, if you have five extra stitches on one side of the neck, try and make sure you have the same number extra on the other side. If you don't have enough stitches on the needles and have already reached the end of the neck, it could be that you are using the incorrect edge stitch.

1 Before you start picking up stitches, divide the edge you are going to pick up along into evenly sized sections. Mark these with loops of contrast yarn. Divide the number of stitches to be picked up by the number of sections you have marked out and you will know how many stitches to pick up in each section.

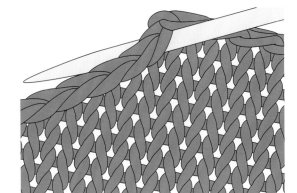

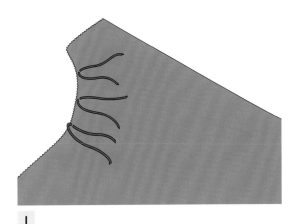

2 Put the tip of a needle into the first row, in the space between the edge stitch and the next stitch.

3 Wrap the yarn around the needle and pull the loop through on the tip of the needle. Pick up one stitch from each row in this way.

4 As the stitches you are picking up are wider than the rows you are picking up from, after every third picked-up stitch, skip one row space.

5 If, when you pick up a stitch you have a hole lying below it or the stitch is very loose, slip the stitch onto a spare needle and knit into the back of it. This will help to close the gap.

6 When you get to the part of the neck where you will knit the stitches left on the holder at the front of the neck, it can be quite a jump from the stitch picked up from the last row. I find it's best to pick up a stitch from one of the vertical stitches to make the neckband fit evenly around the curve.

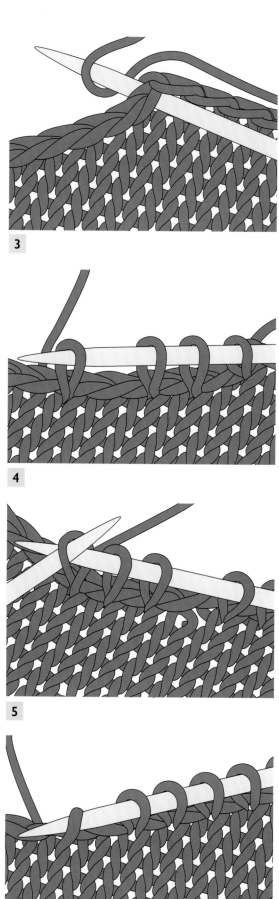

3

4

5

6

INFORMATION

TENSION

Obtaining the correct tension is perhaps the most important single factor which can make the difference between a successful project and a disastrous one. Tension controls both the shape and size of an article, so any variation, however slight, can distort the finished project. We recommend that you knit a square in pattern and/or stocking stitch (depending on the pattern instructions) of perhaps five to ten more stitches and five to ten more rows than those given in the tension note. Mark out the central 10cm/4in square with pins. If you have too many stitches to 10cm/4in, try again using thicker needles. If you have too few stitches to 10cm/4in, try again using finer needles.

FINISHING INSTRUCTIONS

After working for hours knitting a project, it seems a great pity that many projects are spoiled because such little care is taken in the pressing and finishing process. Follow the instructions below for a truly professional-looking garment.

PRESSING

Block out each piece of knitting and following the instructions on the ball band to press the project pieces, omitting the ribs. Tip: Take special care to press the edges, as this will make sewing up both easier and neater. If the ball band indicates that the fabric is not to be pressed, then covering the blocked out fabric with a damp white cotton cloth and leaving it to stand will have the desired effect. Darn in all ends neatly along the selvage edge or a colour join, as appropriate.

STITCHING

When stitching the pieces together, remember to match areas of colour and texture very carefully where they meet. Use a seam stitch such as back stitch or mattress stitch for all main knitting seams and join all ribs and neckband with mattress stitch, unless otherwise stated.

RESOURCES

Yarn
Rowan Yarns *www.knitrowan.com*

Knitting Needles
Milward *www.deramores.com*

Stuffing
John Lewis *www.johnlewis.com*

Buttons
John Lewis *www.johnlewis.com*

Cushion Pads
John Lewis *www.johnlewis.com*

Fabric
John Lewis *www.johnlewis.com*
Cotton Patch *www.cottonpatch.co.uk*

Faux Fur Pompoms
Rowan Yarns *www.knitrowan.com*

ACKNOWLEDGEMENTS

I would like to thank everybody who has helped me bring this book together. Most importantly, my wonderful husband, for putting up with all of the late nights I spent writing it and for supporting me throughout the process. Special thanks also go to the team at Rowan for endorsing my book with yarn sponsorship. Also, I must thank Linda Williams and Daniella Taylor who helped by submitting three of their designs (the tea cosy, lace wrap and chunky lace snood) for use within this book. Finally, I would like to thank the team at GMC and Quail for bringing my ideas to life and making this book possible.

Emma Osmond

INDEX

To order a book, or to request
a catalogue, contact:

GMC Publications Ltd
Castle Place, 166 High Street,
Lewes, East Sussex,
BN7 1XU
United Kingdom
Tel: +44 (0)1273 488005
www.gmcbooks.com